YOLO

summersdale

YOLO

Summersdale Publishers Ltd
46 West Street
Chichester
West Sussex
PO19 1RP
UK

www.summersdale.com

Printed and bound in China

ISBN: 978-1-84953-489-5

Substantial discounts on bulk quantities of Summersdale books are available to corporations, professional associations and other organisations. For details contact Nicky Douglas by telephone: +44 (0) 1243 756902, fax: +44 (0) 1243 786300 or email: nicky@summersdale.com.

INTRODUCTION

Those who say that 'life is not a rehearsal' are absolutely right. You've got to get out there and start seizing the day, because You Only Live Once — and you need something to tweet, blog and update your status about!

From farmers who became presidents to thousand-year-old rays of starlight, and from the largest bubblegum bubble to the 7 octillion little pieces that make you you, this inspiring collection of amazing facts will give you a boost even when your Wi-Fi isn't working.

Stevie Wonder signed his first record contract with Motown at the tender age of 11. #ageisnobarrier

Presidents George Washington and Jimmy Carter both started their careers as farmers.
#mrpresidenthadafarmeieio

#yolo

Amongst Thomas Edison's inventions are wax paper and the dictating machine.
#notjustalightbulbmoment
#mustpatentthat!

#YOLO

Scientists in America have calculated that humans are physically capable of running at up to 40 mph – that's faster than Usain Bolt.
#fasterthanaspeedingbolt

#YOLO

Tea is said to have been discovered by a Chinese emperor in 2737 BC, when some leaves drifted into a pot of water he was boiling. #inspirationstrikesanytime

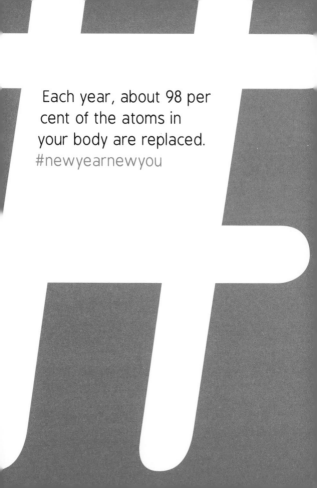

Each year, about 98 per cent of the atoms in your body are replaced.
#newyearnewyou

Born in 1931, Carmen Dell'Orefice is the oldest working model in the world. She started her career at 15. #whosaysyouthisbeauty?

The cruise ship *The World* is the only residential cruise ship in existence, with 165 permanent residents constantly touring the globe.
#bestretirementever

Silly Putty has a specific gravity so close to human skin that doctors have used it to align and test CAT scan machines. #beingadoctorischildsplay

When you receive a
text message on a Nokia
phone, the tone played is
'SMS' in Morse code.
#bipbipbipbeepbeepbipbipbip
#sorryithoughtitwasonsilent

Leonardo da Vinci could draw
with one hand whilst writing
with the other.
#wholenewlevelofmultitasking

Playing a musical instrument can raise your IQ by up to 5 points. Time to get that fiddle or ukulele out! #ifmusicbethefoodofbraininess

As a child, record-breaking circumnavigator Dame Ellen MacArthur saved her school dinner money for three years to buy her first boat. **#italladdsup**

Kissing releases the hormone oxytocin into the body, relieving stress as well as making you feel romantic.
#kissmequick
#orkissmeslowly
#justkissmedammit!

#yolo

Napping for a short time after learning something new can help your memory.
#zzzzzahyesiremember

#YOLO

7,000,000,000,000,000,000,000,000,000 (7 octillion).
That's the number of atoms in your body.
#somanytinypiecesofyou

Sir Isaac Newton invented calculus whilst Cambridge University was closed due to the outbreak of bubonic plague.
#ifyouneeditinventit
#geniushappensanywhere

Artist Guido Daniele
creates incredibly
detailed images of
animals, using hands
as his canvas.
#bodybeautiful
#whoneedspaper

German designer Anke Domaske has proved you can repurpose anything by creating a fibre made entirely from milk — she calls it Qmilch.
#softandflowy

An ice cream parlour in Missouri solved the local cicada overpopulation by making cicada ice cream. #thatsnotachocolatechip!

Finland has 180,000
islands – enough for
one for every
30 people.
#visiteachandeveryone

A person will, on average,
have over 1,500 dreams
each year.
#letsmakesomecometrue

John Major left school in 1959 aged 16, with only three O-levels.
He went on to serve as Prime Minister for seven years.

#whereveryoustartyoucangoanywhere

Wearing tight trousers can make men become impotent.
#hipstersbeware
#hanglooseandmultiply

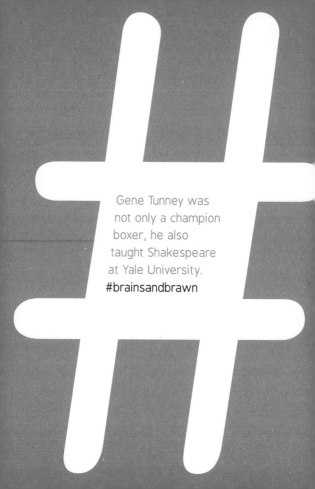

Gene Tunney was
not only a champion
boxer, he also
taught Shakespeare
at Yale University.
#brainsandbrawn

Half of the world's oxygen supply comes from the Amazon rainforest.
#savetheforestbreatheeasy

#yolo

NASA have a new service called 'spot the space station'. Sign up and they will send you a text or email when the International Space Station is due to fly over your head.
#betterthanwhereswally

#YOLO

The world's oldest tree,
Old Tjikko, is in Sweden,
and is 9,550 years old.
#yourenotasoldasyouthink
#9550isthenew30

#YOLO

Bryan Berg built the world's largest playing card structure, modelling three Macau hotels entirely from cards: 218,792 of them.
#creativityiseverywhere
#houseofcards

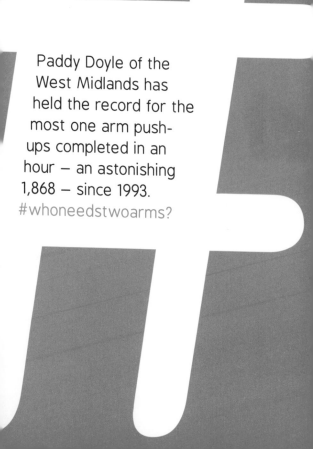

Paddy Doyle of the West Midlands has held the record for the most one arm push-ups completed in an hour — an astonishing 1,868 — since 1993.
#whoneedstwoarms?

The word 'checkmate' comes from the Persian *Shah mat*, meaning 'the King is dead'. #longlivethequeen

The cells in your
tastebuds have a
lifespan of ten days.
#isthatwhytasteschange?

There are 1,665 steps to the top of the Eiffel Tower. #worththeclimb #stopforabreatherthough!

Elephants without tusks
are evolving as a genetic
response to poaching.
#seethemwhileyoucan

An elephant's pregnancy lasts
two years.
#makesninemonthsseemshort!

The ideal length of time for a nap
is 26 minutes.
#timetostartpractisingnapskills

When you step forward, you are using up to 200 muscles.
#incredibleyou

Clyde William Tombaugh, the man who discovered Pluto, died in 1997. An ounce of his ashes are on their way to Pluto aboard the New Horizons space probe.
#livethedreamevenindeath
#afittingend

#yolo

Only one per cent of people
are born with red hair.
#ifyouvegotitflauntit

#YOLO

The human eye can detect
10,000,000 different colours.
#helpsyouchoosethatperfectshade

#YOLO

Leonardo da Vinci
invented the parachute
long before we took
to the skies in planes.
#notcrazybutvisionary

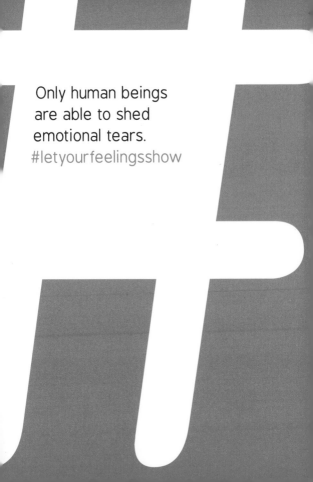

Only human beings
are able to shed
emotional tears.
#letyourfeelingsshow

The Bootleg Beatles, arguably the most successful Beatles tribute band, have had a career three times longer than the actual Beatles! #stayingpower #thetributethatkeepsgiving

If you measured the energy from the sun in the same way that you measure the energy from a lightbulb, it would be 368 billion billion megawatts. #thatsamightybigbulb

Apollo 11 had only 20 seconds worth of fuel left when it landed. #allswellthatendswell

Paris is home to more dogs than people.
#perfectgetawayfordoglovers

Bertrand Bookshop in Lisbon,
Portugal, has been open since
1732, making it the oldest
bookshop in the world.
#sowtheseedsofsomethinglasting

Though there are sharks in the seas around Bermuda, nobody has ever been killed by a shark there.
#idealholidaydestination

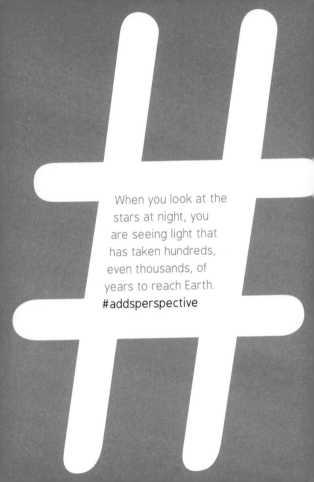

When you look at the stars at night, you are seeing light that has taken hundreds, even thousands, of years to reach Earth. #addsperspective

There is a town in
Norway called Hell.
#whenhellfreezesover
#nextwinterthen?

#yolo

According to Hasbro, the longest ever game of Monopoly took an astounding 70 days.
#christmasdaygamesareshorter
#believeitornot

#YOLO

The average human being will take 216,262,500 steps in a lifetime.
#timetobuyapedometer?

The reason the first CDs were designed to hold 74 minutes of music is that Beethoven's 9th Symphony is that length.
#techieswithsoul
#beethoven:stillhip

Since she appeared in 1959, Barbie has had 125 different careers.
#theoriginalcareergirl
#itsoktochangeyourmind

The longest note ever played on a saxophone lasted for 45 minutes. #extraordinarylungpower #takeadeepbreath

Erika La Tour Eiffel, a woman who lives in San Francisco, is married to the Eiffel Tower.
#toweringromance
#followyourheart

Brad Pitt's job before becoming an actor was dancing around in a chicken suit to draw people to a chicken restaurant. #anystartisagoodstart

Crows are extremely clever:
they can solve problems and
even make and use tools.
#birdbraincouldbeacompliment

Women's hearts tend to beat more quickly than men's.
#andherheartskippedabeat

In Hong Kong, you can buy
bottles of soft drink that freeze
themselves.
#literallysupercool

An 'eco' mobile phone
has been designed
which runs on the sugar
in fizzy drinks.
#sweettechnology

Your birthday is shared with about 9 million other people around the world. #letshaveaparty!

#yolo

You burn more calories when asleep than you do whilst watching TV.
#tosleepperchancetoslim

You weigh slightly less when the moon is directly overhead, due to its gravitational pull.
#theallnewmoondiet

Jackie Chan was born after 12 months in the womb, weighing 12 pounds.
#worthwaitingfor

Leonard Cohen's original version of *Hallelujah* had more than 80 verses.

#epicsongster

The longest continuous
Frisbee game in history
lasted 126 hours.
#largescalededication

Even the Queen uses email. She sent her first one in 1976.
#aheadofthetimes

The only national football team that has not lost against Brazil at some time is Norway.
#maybetheyllwinnexttime

Elephants have self-awareness – they can recognise themselves in a mirror.
#doesmytrunklookbiginthis?

The founder of Fender guitars,
Leo Fender, could not play guitar.
In fact, he was a saxophonist.
#dowhatyoulovelovewhatyoudo

Samuel Morse, inventor of
the Morse code, was also
an accomplished painter.
#icallthispiecedotdotdotdashdash

No member of the
Beatles was able to
read music, yet they
are one of the most
influential bands of
all time.
#feelvsskill

You are more likely to get germs from someone by shaking their hand than from kissing them.
#tipsfornextbusinessmeeting

#yolo

Mount Everest has 3G coverage.
#guesswhereiam?

#YOLO

A 13-year-old British boy was struck by lightning at 13:13 on Friday 13. He survived.
#unluckyforsome

#YOLO

The song *Yesterday*
was performed 7 million
times in the 20th century.
#anoldiebutagoodie

The most pierced woman in the world lives in Scotland. According to *Guinness World Records*, she has 462 piercings, and has been pierced 4,225 times.

#heavymetal

Among other things, porpois
teeth, woodpecker scalps
and giraffe tails have all
been used as money.
#moneyisnteverything
#butitcanbeanything

The name Elvis Presley
appears on the UK
electoral register
22 times.
#longlivetheking!
#heisstillwithus

Though it would be possible to live without bacteria, we would have to eat a special diet as bacteria are essential for normal digestion.
#lovethelittlefellas
#onlydoingtheirjob

In 2011, there were 3.1 billion registered email accounts in the world.

#itsgoodtoemail

American Chad Fell holds the record for the largest bubblegum bubble blown. It was larger than a basketball, with a diameter of 50.8 cm.
#imforeverblowingbubbles

In October 2012, street artist
Megx transformed a bridge in
Wuppertal, Germany, into Lego
bricks using coloured panels.
#youreallycanbuildanything
#changeyourworldview

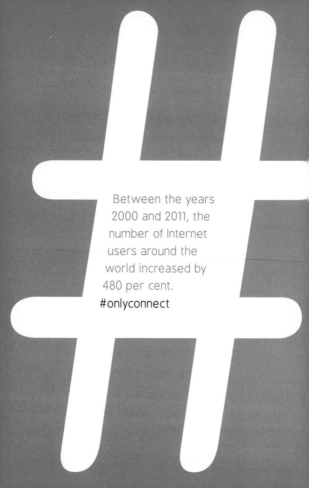

Between the years 2000 and 2011, the number of Internet users around the world increased by 480 per cent.
#onlyconnect

Each day, about 150 couples get married in Las Vegas.
#feelthelove

#yolo

Plants will grow faster
when played music.
#thegreenhousesoundsnicetoo

#YOLO

There are ten times as
many bacterial cells in your
body as human cells.
#whoami
#lovethegermsyoulivewith

A bottle of champagne contain around 100 million bubbles.
#nowonderitmakesyougiddy

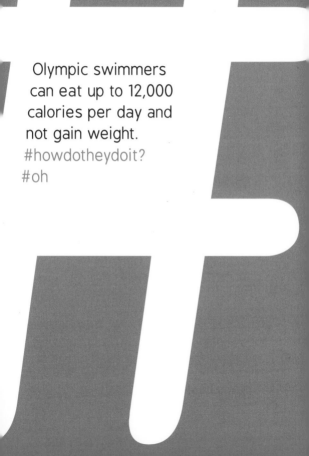

Olympic swimmers can eat up to 12,000 calories per day and not gain weight.
#howdotheydoit?
#oh

Lake Retba, or *Lac Rose*, in Senegal has pink water due to a particular type of algae. It is also highly salty and easy to float in. #liebackandwatchtheclouds

Your bones are
stronger than concrete.
#betternottestthisthough

If you're interested in finding out
more about our books,
find us on Facebook at
Summersdale Publishers
and follow us on Twitter at
@Summersdale.

www.summersdale.com